WITHDRAWN

D1472678

INSIDE THE NFL

Buffalo Bills

BY
ZACH WYNER

MEDIA ENHANCED BOOKS
AV²
BY WEIGL™
ADDED VALUE • AUDIO VISUAL

AV² provides enriched content that supplements and complements this book. Weigl's AV² books strive to create inspired learning and engage young minds in a total learning experience.

Your AV² Media Enhanced books come alive with...

Audio
Listen to sections of the book read aloud.

Key Words
Study vocabulary, and complete a matching word activity.

Video
Watch informative video clips.

Quizzes
Test your knowledge.

Go to **www.av2books.com**, and enter this book's unique code.

Embedded Weblinks
Gain additional information for research.

Slide Show
View images and captions, and prepare a presentation.

BOOK CODE

H 5 4 0 8 5 4

Try This!
Complete activities and hands-on experiments.

... and much, much more!

AV² by Weigl brings you media enhanced books that support active learning.

Published by AV² by Weigl
350 5th Avenue, 59th Floor
New York, NY 10118
Websites: www.av2books.com   www.weigl.com

Library of Congress Control Number: 2014931145

ISBN 978-1-4896-0794-2 (hardcover)
ISBN 978-1-4896-0796-6 (single-user eBook)
ISBN 978-1-4896-0797-3 (multi-user eBook)

Printed in the United States of America in North Mankato, Minnesota
1 2 3 4 5 6 7 8 9 0   18 17 16 15 14

042014
WEP150314

Project Coordinator Aaron Carr
Art Director Terry Paulhus

Photo Credits
Every reasonable effort has been made to trace ownership and to obtain permission to reprint copyright material. The publishers would be pleased to have any errors or omissions brought to their attention so that they may be corrected in subsequent printings.

Weigl acknowledges Getty Images as its primary image supplier for this title.

Buffalo Bills

CONTENTS

Introduction

The Buffalo Bills are located in the northernmost city in the American Football Conference (AFC). Far from the bright lights of Manhattan, the city of Buffalo, New York, is nestled on the shore of Lake Erie, about 25 miles (40 kilometers) from the Canadian border. While it is the second largest city in New York State, it is much smaller, colder, and quieter than New York City. However, firing up Buffalo residents is not hard. Put some chicken wings on the table and a Bills game on the TV, and these quiet folks get plenty loud.

For many years the Bills were a dominant force in the NFL. They made the playoffs 13 times between 1974 and 1999 and made four straight trips to the **Super Bowl** in the early 1990s.

The charging bison worn by the Buffalo Bills is based on the one used by Howard University in Washington, D.C.

Unfortunately, hard times in recent years have kept Bills fans from a chance to cheer their team to **postseason** glory. However, with the signing of a new coach and a fresh assortment of gifted players, the Bills hope to once again bring the warmth of winning to their chilly city.

EJ Manuel is the current starting quarterback of the Bills. He was drafted by Buffalo in 2013.

BILLS

Stadium Ralph Wilson Stadium

Division American Football Conference (AFC) East

Head coach Doug Marrone

Location Buffalo, New York

Super Bowl titles 0

Nicknames None

17
Playoff Appearances

4
Conference Championships

10
Division Championships

History

The Buffalo Bills' name is partially inspired by "Buffalo Bill" Cody, a showman from the

WILD WEST.

⊔ By all measures, Jim Kelly was the best quarterback to ever play for the Bills. He was inducted into the Pro Football Hall of Fame in 2002.

A founding member of the American Football League (AFL), the Buffalo Bills were two-time AFL champions. From 1963 to 1966, they made the playoffs four straight times and won back-to-back titles in 1964 and 1965. Eight Bills made the 1964 AFL All-Star team and three were named to the AFL's All-Time team. Quarterback Jack Kemp is credited for leading the Bills on and off the field.

After the AFL/NFL **merger** in 1970, the Bills were defined by a running game that ranks as one of the greatest of all time. Hall of famer Joe DeLamielleure captained an offensive line known as "The Electric Company." Behind these impressive giants, running back O.J. Simpson, or "the Juice" as he was often called, set numerous rushing records. The Electric Company's nickname was created because they helped "turn on the Juice."

The Bills' fortunes improved dramatically when they named Marv Levy their head coach in 1986. In 12 years at the helm, Levy coached hall of famers Thurman Thomas, Jim Kelly, and Bruce Smith to six division titles and four Super Bowl appearances. The 1990 Bills, with nine **Pro Bowlers** and Defensive Player of the Year Smith, suffered a heartbreaking 20-19 Super Bowl loss that symbolized an era of near misses.

⊔ Thurman Thomas played his final season with the Miami Dolphins. However, at the very end of his career, he signed a one-day contract with Buffalo so he could retire as a Bill.

The Stadium

Ralph Wilson Stadium can seat 73,967 fans.

The Bills spent their first 13 seasons at War Memorial Stadium, also known as "The Rockpile." Then, the team moved into Ralph Wilson Stadium in Orchard Park, a suburb of Buffalo. The new open-air stadium allowed for nearly 30,000 more fans to watch their beloved Bills. Other amenities added to the stadium included more **luxury boxes** and a new high definition Mitsubishi LED scoreboard measuring 88.8 feet by 32.5 feet (27 by 10 meters).

Buffalo Bills fans go to great lengths to show their team spirit.

Kickers face the greatest challenge at Ralph Wilson Stadium. Downwind of Lake Erie, Buffalo is one of the windiest cities in the country. In addition to this, the stadium is built 60 feet below ground level. The result is that wind can drop into the stadium and knock a football off course.

The Bills have a terrific postseason record at Ralph Wilson Stadium. After beating the Houston Oilers there in 1989, they won every postseason contest played at home until being defeated in 1996 by the Jacksonville Jaguars.

While attending a game at Ralph Wilson Stadium, fans fill their bellies with a "Beef on Weck" sandwich made with rare roast beef, heated au jus, kosher salt, caraway seeds, and horseradish.

Where They Play

CANADA

Washington | 30

Oregon

Montana

Idaho

North Dakota

Minnesota

Lake Superior

23 → Wisconsin

22

29

South Dakota

Wyoming

Nevada

14

Iowa

24

Illinois

15

Utah

Nebraska

13

16

California

Colorado

Kansas

Missouri

31

UNITED STATES

Arizona

New Mexico

Oklahoma

Arkansas

32

17

Texas

Mississippi

Louisiana

12

27

Pacific Ocean

Alaska

Hawai'i

MEXICO

Gulf of Mexico

0   500 Miles
0   500 km

0   100 Miles
0   100 km

AMERICAN FOOTBALL CONFERENCE

EAST
1   Gillette Stadium
2   MetLife Stadium
★ 3   Ralph Wilson Stadium
4   Sun Life Stadium

NORTH
5   FirstEnergy Stadium
6   Heinz Field
7   M&T Bank Stadium
8   Paul Brown Stadium

SOUTH
9   EverBank Field
10 LP Field
11 Lucas Oil Stadium
12 NRG Stadium

WEST
13 Arrowhead Stadium
14 Sports Authority Field at Mile High
15 O.co Coliseum
16 Qualcomm Stadium

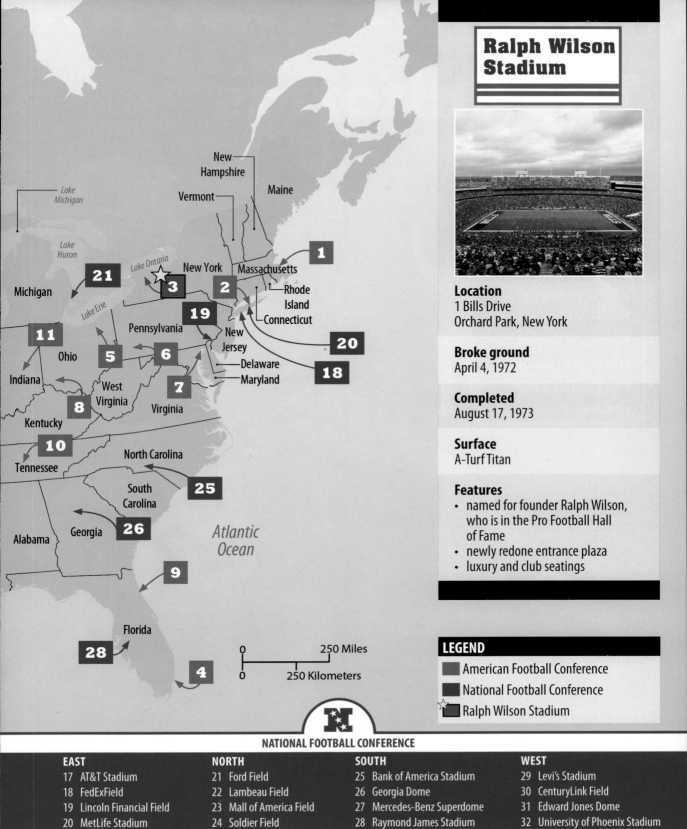

Location
1 Bills Drive
Orchard Park, New York

Broke ground
April 4, 1972

Completed
August 17, 1973

Surface
A-Turf Titan

Features
- named for founder Ralph Wilson, who is in the Pro Football Hall of Fame
- newly redone entrance plaza
- luxury and club seatings

LEGEND
- American Football Conference
- National Football Conference
- Ralph Wilson Stadium

NATIONAL FOOTBALL CONFERENCE

EAST	NORTH	SOUTH	WEST
17 AT&T Stadium	21 Ford Field	25 Bank of America Stadium	29 Levi's Stadium
18 FedExField	22 Lambeau Field	26 Georgia Dome	30 CenturyLink Field
19 Lincoln Financial Field	23 Mall of America Field	27 Mercedes-Benz Superdome	31 Edward Jones Dome
20 MetLife Stadium	24 Soldier Field	28 Raymond James Stadium	32 University of Phoenix Stadium

The Uniforms

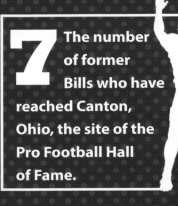

7 The number of former Bills who have reached Canton, Ohio, the site of the Pro Football Hall of Fame.

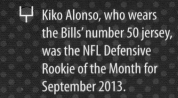 Kiko Alonso, who wears the Bills' number 50 jersey, was the NFL Defensive Rookie of the Month for September 2013.

Throughout the years, the Bills' uniforms have undergone many subtle changes, but red, white, and blue have always been the primary colors. The home jersey has always been blue, with white jerseys being worn on rare occasions. Pants have changed from blue to white, but have always had blue, red, and white stripes down the sides.

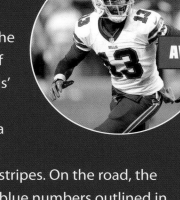

HOME

AWAY

After a period in the 2000s that saw the uniforms change to a darker shade of blue with nickel-grey accents, the Bills' current uniforms are modeled after those of the late 1970s. They feature a lighter shade of blue, white numbers, white pants, and red, white, and blue stripes. On the road, the Bills currently wear white jerseys with blue numbers outlined in red, and white pants with blue and red stripes.

NFL players need to move quickly and easily on the field. NFL uniforms are designed to be comfortable, yet durable.

The Helmets

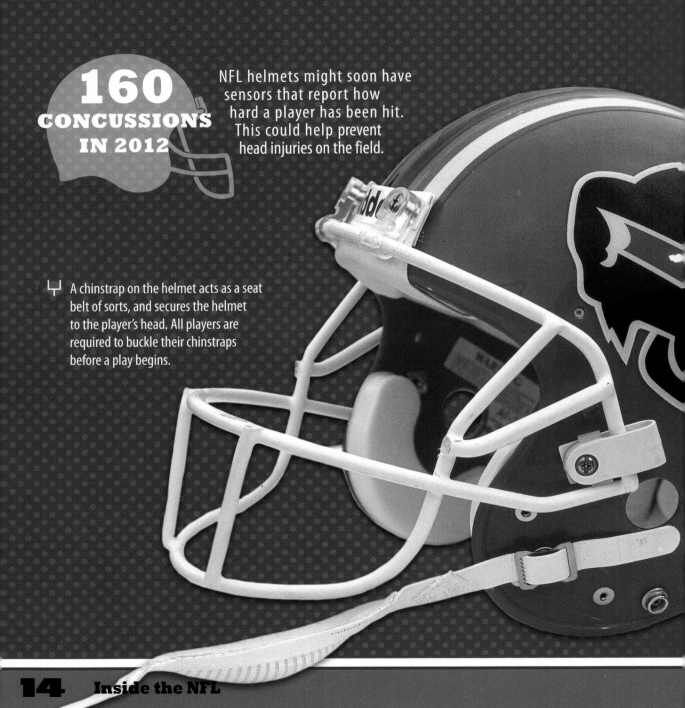

160 CONCUSSIONS IN 2012

NFL helmets might soon have sensors that report how hard a player has been hit. This could help prevent head injuries on the field.

A chinstrap on the helmet acts as a seat belt of sorts, and secures the helmet to the player's head. All players are required to buckle their chinstraps before a play begins.

The Buffalo Bills' original helmets were silver with blue numbers on the side. In 1962, the Bills debuted white helmets with a red standing bison **logo** and a red stripe down the center. In 1974, the change from "standing" bison to "charging" bison was made. The charging bison was blue with a red stripe extending from its horn, making it appear swift and ferocious. This change was fitting, considering it was made during an era in which "The Electric Company" was clearing gaping holes in opposing defensive lines and the Bills were setting NFL rushing records.

From 1984 to 2010, the Bills' primary helmet color was red. This change was made partly to help their quarterbacks differentiate between receivers and defenders. In 2011, the Bills changed back to a white helmet with a red and blue stripe down the middle and a blue charging bison. The original red standing bison adorns the team's alternate jerseys.

Football is a very physical sport. Helmets, as well as leg and shoulder pads, are required to keep players safe.

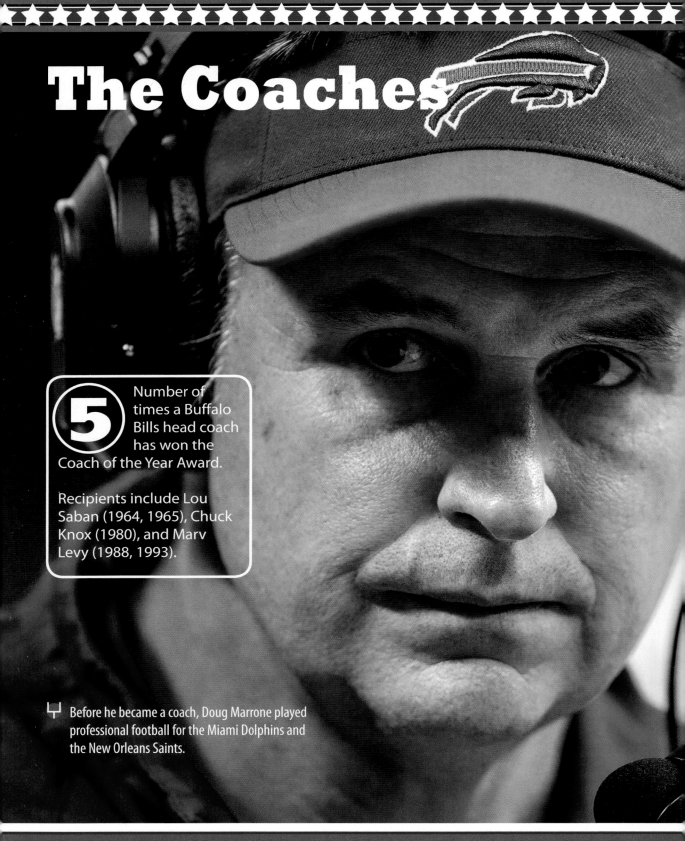

The Coaches

5 Number of times a Buffalo Bills head coach has won the Coach of the Year Award.

Recipients include Lou Saban (1964, 1965), Chuck Knox (1980), and Marv Levy (1988, 1993).

Before he became a coach, Doug Marrone played professional football for the Miami Dolphins and the New Orleans Saints.

From the beginning, the coaching bar in Buffalo was set very high. Lou Saban coached the Bills to back-to-back AFL titles in 1964–1965, and won two Coach of the Year awards. Since he left the team, many outstanding football minds have come to Buffalo to repeat his success. Included on this list are two Coach of the Year Award winners and one member of the NFL hall of fame.

CHUCK KNOX

When Chuck Knox came to the Bills in 1978, they had won just five of their previous 28 games. By 1980, the Bills improved to 11-5, running the ball an average of 38 times per game. Buffalo won the AFC East, and Knox was named Coach of the Year that season.

MARV LEVY

Marv Levy had 30 years of coaching experience before he joined the Bills in 1986. He coached them to eight playoff appearances in 12 years. Behind his high-octane **"no huddle" offense**, the Bills reached four Super Bowls in a row. Levy is the most successful coach in Bills history.

DOUG MARRONE

Doug Marrone's 20 years of college and NFL coaching experience includes three years in New Orleans from 2006 to 2008. During that time, he turned the Saints' offense into the highest-scoring in the NFL. Bills fans hope he has the same influence on quarterback EJ Manuel that he had on Saints quarterback Drew Brees.

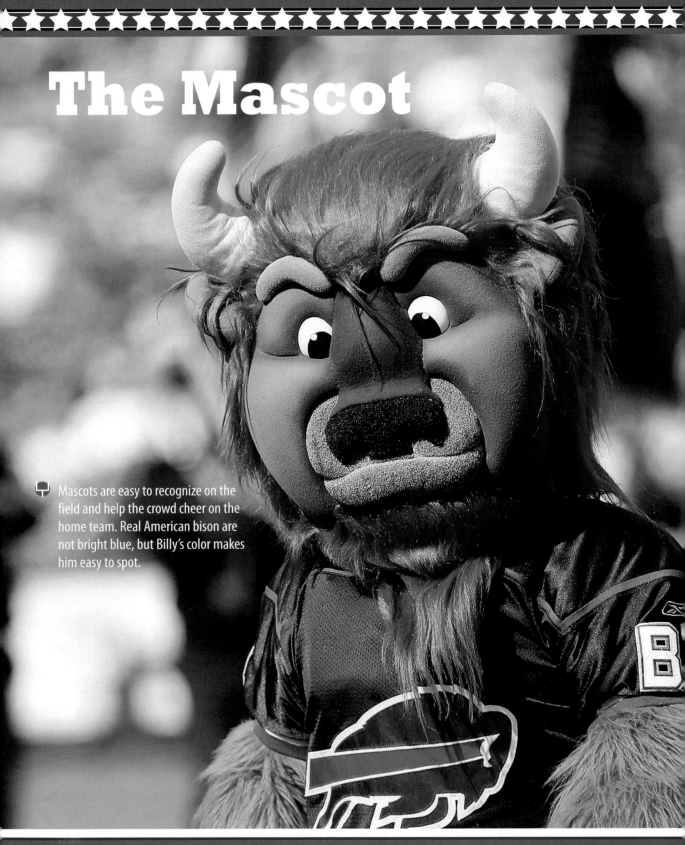

The Mascot

Mascots are easy to recognize on the field and help the crowd cheer on the home team. Real American bison are not bright blue, but Billy's color makes him easy to spot.

Born on September 3, 2000, William "Billy" the Buffalo is a towering presence on the Buffalo Bills sideline. He is an eight-foot-tall blue buffalo who wears the letters "BB" on his Bills jersey. While Billy is still very young, he is a tremendously hard worker. Besides cheering his heart out at Bills games, he makes numerous public appearances every year. When not revving up crowds and cheering on his team, Billy visits schools and hospitals and attends charitable events.

A graduate of **Bovine** University, this resident of Orchard Park says his career goals include making his mother proud and cheering the Bills all the way to the Super Bowl.

Billy's hobbies include playing for 60 minutes a day, signing autographs, taking photos, and visiting Bills fans everywhere.

Billy's favorite foods are fruit, vegetables, and Buffalo chicken wings.

Legends of the Past

Many great players have suited up in the Bills' blue and red. A few of them have become icons of the team and the city it represents.

Bruce Smith

Known as "The Sack Man" at Virginia Tech University, Bruce Smith kept right on terrorizing quarterbacks in the NFL. In 15 years with the Buffalo Bills, he made 11 Pro Bowls and was twice named Defensive Player of the Year (1990, 1996). His dominance took center stage during Super Bowl XXV, when he sacked quarterback Jeff Hostetler to force a safety and stopped the Giants in the **backfield** on a fourth down to force a turnover. Smith retired in 2003 with 200 career sacks, making "The Sack Man" number one on the NFL's all-time list.

Position Defensive End
Seasons 19 (1985–2003)
Born June 18, 1963, in Norfolk, Virginia

Thurman Thomas

During the Bills run of four-straight Super Bowl appearances, Thurman Thomas was their most reliable offensive weapon. Thomas combined great speed, agility, vision, and was a terrific receiver out of the backfield. For four straight seasons from 1989 to 1992, Thomas led the NFL in **yards from scrimmage**, averaging 125 yards per game. He dominated the NY Giants defense in Super Bowl XXV, rushing for 135 yards and a touchdown and catching five passes for 55 yards. The NFL's Most Valuable Player in 1991. Thomas was elected to the Pro Football Hall of Fame in 2007.

Position Running Back
Seasons 13 (1988–2000)
Born May 16, 1966, in Houston, Texas

Jim Kelly

Jim Kelly was the third quarterback selected in the 1983 **NFL Draft**, which included hall of famers Dan Marino and John Elway. The quarterback of Marv Levy's "no huddle" offense, Kelly's best years in the NFL came in the early 1990s when he piloted one of the best offenses in the league. In 1990, he led the NFL in **passer rating** (101) and completion percentage (63), and in 1991, he led all quarterbacks in touchdowns (33). In 11 seasons with the Bills, hall of famer Jim Kelly led his team to the playoffs eight times, won 11 postseason games, and four AFC Championships.

Position Quarterback
Seasons 11 (1986–1996)
Born February 14, 1960, in East Brady, Pennsylvania

Andre Reed

On January 3, 1993, the Bills trailed 35-3 in the third quarter of a playoff game against the Houston Oilers. What happened next was something that Bills fans remember like it was yesterday. The Bills scored 35 points and won the game in overtime 41-38. Andre Reed's three touchdown catches were instrumental in the game that NFL fans simply call "The Comeback." Over the course of Reed's marvelous career, he was selected to seven Pro Bowls and was a four-time AFC Champion. His 951 career receptions place him 10th on the NFL's all-time list.

Position Wide Receiver
Seasons 16 (1985–2000)
Born January 29, 1964, in Allentown, Pennsylvania

Stars of Today

Today's Bills team is made up of many young, talented players who have proven that they are among the best players in the league.

Mario Williams

With the first pick in the 2006 NFL Draft, the Houston Texans selected 6-foot, 7-inch, 295-pound Mario Williams. Having awed scouts with a 40.5-inch (102.8-centimeter) vertical leap and 35 bench-press reps of 225 pounds (102 kilograms), in 2008, Williams proved himself worthy of their esteem, making his first of two consecutive Pro Bowls. In 2011, Williams signed a six-year deal with the Buffalo Bills that made him the highest paid player in franchise history. Early in 2013, he broke the franchise record with 4.5 sacks in a single game, showing fans he was worth the investment.

Position Defensive End
Seasons 8 (2006–2013)
Born January 31, 1985, in Richlands, North Carolina

Kiko Alonso

In 2012, Kiko Alonso was a star linebacker for the University of Oregon Ducks. Coming off a season in which he had been Oregon's eighth-leading tackler, Alonso emerged as a leader, recording 87 total tackles, 16 tackles for loss, one sack, four interceptions, seven pass deflections, and two forced fumbles. Alonso's rapid development and early success at the professional level have made him an important part of the Buffalo Bills' future. Alonso broke the 100-tackle mark in his 11th NFL game.

Position Linebacker
Seasons 1 (2013)
Born August 14, 1990, in Newton, Massachusetts

EJ Manuel

E J Manuel was the first quarterback taken in the 2012 NFL Draft. Having spent the previous two seasons leading the Florida State Seminoles back to national prominence, Manuel was seen by many as the top quarterback prospect because of his leadership, size, arm strength, and speed. Manuel can break down a defense in a number of different ways, and in his first season with the Bills, he wasted little time in demonstrating his potential. In his first two games as a pro, Manuel completed 45 of 66 passes, or 68 percent, for 446 yards and three touchdowns.

Position Quarterback
Seasons 1 (2013)
Born March 19, 1990, in Virginia Beach, Virginia

Stevie Johnson

K nown for his creative touchdown celebrations and his ability to take over a game, Stevie Johnson is one of rookie quarterback EJ Manuel's most dangerous weapons. Combining size, strength, speed, and crisp route running, Johnson is both consistent and capable of the big play. Johnson's finest season came in 2010, when he caught 82 passes in just 13 games for 1,073 yards and 10 touchdowns. In 2012, Johnson became the first Bills receiver ever to record more than 1,000 receiving yards in three consecutive seasons.

Position Wide Receiver
Seasons 6 (2008–2013)
Born July 22, 1986, in San Francisco, California

All-Time Records

11,938 Career Rushing Yards

In 12 seasons with the Bills, Thurman Thomas broke the 1,000-yard mark eight times on the way to becoming the Bills all-time rushing leader.

171 Career Sacks

Bruce Smith's 171 sacks in a Buffalo Bills uniform are a team record. Smith recorded another 29 sacks with the Washington Redskins to bring his career total to an NFL-record 200.

112
All-time Coaching Wins

Hall of fame coach Marv Levy spent 47 years coaching football. In 12 seasons with the Bills, he won a franchise-record number of games.

4,359
Single-season Passing Yards

Former New England Patriot Drew Bledsoe spent the final five seasons of his NFL career in Buffalo, breaking the franchise's single-season passing record in 2002.

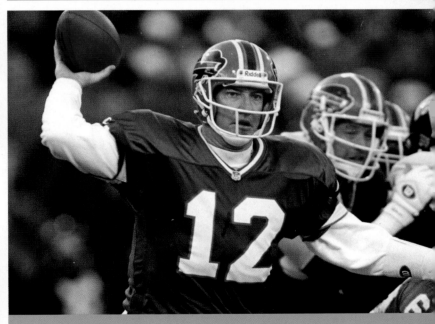

35,467
Career Passing Yards

While he never broke the 4,000-yard mark in a season, Jim Kelly passed for more than 3,000 yards eight times in his hall of fame career.

Timeline

Throughout the team's history, the Buffalo Bills have had many memorable events that have become defining moments for the team and its fans.

1960
Named for the famed soldier, bison hunter, and showman "Buffalo Bill" Cody, the Buffalo Bills are original members of the American Football League (AFL).

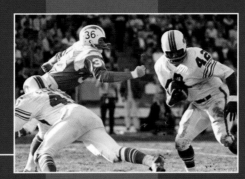

1965
The Bills repeat as AFL champions, defeating the San Diego Chargers 23-0 in the title game. The Bills' defense sets a franchise record by not allowing a rushing touchdown in 17-straight games dating back to the previous season.

In 1970, the AFL and NFL merge, and the Bills are placed in the AFC East division.

| 1960 | 1965 | 1970 | 1975 | 1980 | 1985 |

1986
The Bills sign Jim Kelly. Midway through the season, the Bills hire head coach Marv Levy. Levy constructs his offense around Kelly, Andre Reed, and a talented offensive line. Anchoring the defense is first-round draft pick Bruce Smith.

1962
After leading the San Diego Chargers to back-to-back AFL title games, Jack Kemp is placed on waivers because of an injured hand. This means that another team could sign him. The Buffalo Bills snatch him up and build an offense around their first star quarterback.

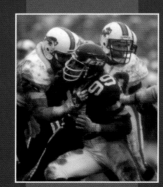

December 27, 1981
The Bills win their first playoff game against their division rival New York Jets. Frank Lewis and Joe Cribbs star as the Bills offense explodes for 31 points. The next week, they are eliminated by the eventual AFC Champion Cincinnati Bengals.

1993
Led by Pro Bowlers Thurman Thomas, Andre Reed, Steve Tasker, Nate Odomes, and Bruce Smith, the Bills win their fifth AFC East division title in six years. They advance to the Super Bowl for an NFL-record fourth straight year, but fall to the Dallas Cowboys 52-17.

The Future
For the Buffalo Bills and their fans, the future has to be brighter than the recent past. The Bills are the only team left in the NFL that has not qualified for the playoffs in the 21st century. The time has come for Bills veterans and coaches to instill their young talent with the confidence to go places this team has not gone in years.

In 2011, the Bills changed their logo back from a "standing" bison to a "charging" bison.

| 1990 | 1995 | 2000 | 2005 | 2010 | 2015 |

In 1999, Doug Flutie carries the Bills to an 11–5 record and a playoff birth.

1990
The Bills score 95 points in their first two playoff games and make their first Super Bowl behind Defensive Player of the Year Bruce Smith. In the Super Bowl, Bills kicker Scott Norwood's 47-yard field goal misses wide right as time expires and the Bills lose a heartbreaker 20-19.

January 1, 2013
Team founder and owner Ralph Wilson, who passed away in 2014, hands over control of football operations to Russ Brandon. Within five days, the Bills hire Doug Marrone as their new head coach, and in April, the team drafts standouts EJ Manuel and Kiko Alonso.

Write a Biography

Life Story

A person's life story can be the subject of a book. This kind of book is called a biography. Biographies often describe the lives of people who have achieved great success. These people may be alive today, or they may have lived many years ago. Reading a biography can help you learn more about a great person.

Get the Facts

Use this book, and research in the library and on the Internet, to find out more about your favorite Bill. Learn as much about this player as you can. What position does he play? What are his statistics in important categories? Has he set any records? Also, be sure to write down key events in the person's life. What was his childhood like? What has he accomplished off the field? Is there anything else that makes this person special or unusual?

Use the Concept Web

A concept web is a useful research tool. Read the questions in the concept web on the following page. Answer the questions in your notebook. Your answers will help you write a biography.

Concept Web

Adulthood
- Where does this individual currently reside?
- Does he or she have a family?

Your Opinion
- What did you learn from the books you read in your research?
- Would you suggest these books to others?
- Was anything missing from these books?

Childhood
- Where and when was this person born?
- Describe his or her parents, siblings, and friends.
- Did this person grow up in unusual circumstances?

Accomplishments off the Field
- What is this person's life's work?
- Has he or she received awards or recognition for accomplishments?
- How have this person's accomplishments served others?

Write a Biography

Help and Obstacles
- Did this individual have a positive attitude?
- Did he or she receive help from others?
- Did this person have a mentor?
- Did this person face any hardships?
- If so, how were the hardships overcome?

Accomplishments on the Field
- What records does this person hold?
- What key games and plays have defined his or her career?
- What are his or her stats in categories important to his or her position?

Work and Preparation
- What was this person's education?
- What was his or her work experience?
- How does this person work; what is the process he or she uses?

Trivia Time

Take this quiz to test your knowledge of the Buffalo Bills. The answers are printed upside-down under each question.

1 Which Bills defensive end is the NFL's all-time leader in sacks?

A. Bruce Smith

2 What nickname was given to the Buffalo Bills' offensive line in the 1970s?

A. The Electric Company

3 In the 1990s, how many straight Super Bowls did the Bills reach?

A. Four

4 How many AFL Championships did the Bills win?

A. Two

5 What was the nickname given to Buffalo's War Memorial Stadium?

A. "The Rockpile"

6 In what league were the Bills original members?

A. American Football League (AFL)

7 Which Buffalo Bill running back took home the NFL's MVP trophy in 1991?

A. Thurman Thomas

8 How many games did the Bills win under Coach Marv Levy?

A. 112

9 Who is the Bills all-time leader in passing yards?

A. Jim Kelly

10 Who coached the Bills to back-to-back AFL titles?

A. Lou Saban

Key Words

backfield: the area of play behind either the offensive or defensive line

bovine: an animal of the cattle group, which also includes buffaloes and bison

logo: a symbol that stands for a team or organization

luxury boxes: a special section of seats in a stadium that usually has the best views of the game

merger: a combination of two things, especially companies, into one

NFL Draft: an annual event where the NFL chooses college football players to be new team members

no huddle offense: an offensive style in which the offensive team avoids delays between plays

passer rating: a rating given to quarterbacks that tries to measure how well they perform on the field

postseason: a sporting event that takes place after the end of the regular season

Pro Bowl: the annual all-star game for NFL players pitting the best players in the National Football Conference against the best players in the American Football Conference

sack: a sack occurs when the quarterback is tackled behind the line of scrimmage before he can throw a forward pass

scrimmage: the yard-line on the field from which the play starts

Super Bowl: the NFL's annual championship game between the winning team from the NFC and the winning team from the AFC

yards from scrimmage: the total of rushing yards and receiving yards

Index

Log on to www.av2books.com

AV² by Weigl brings you media enhanced books that support active learning. Go to www.av2books.com, and enter the special code found on page 2 of this book. You will gain access to enriched and enhanced content that supplements and complements this book. Content includes video, audio, weblinks, quizzes, a slide show, and activities.

AV² Online Navigation

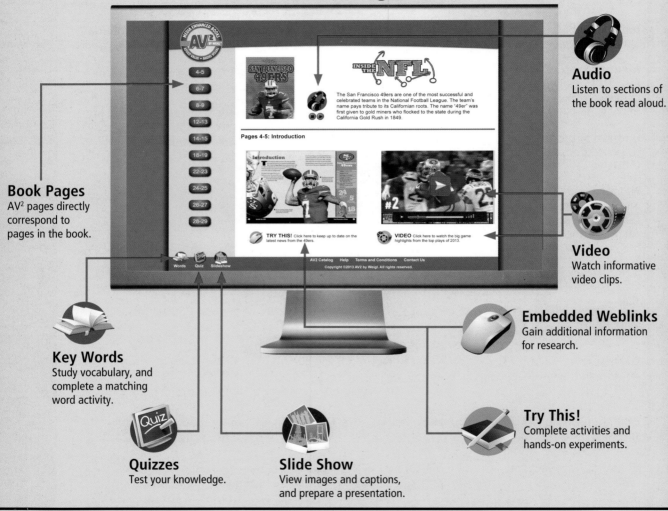

Audio
Listen to sections of the book read aloud.

Book Pages
AV² pages directly correspond to pages in the book.

Video
Watch informative video clips.

Key Words
Study vocabulary, and complete a matching word activity.

Embedded Weblinks
Gain additional information for research.

Quizzes
Test your knowledge.

Slide Show
View images and captions, and prepare a presentation.

Try This!
Complete activities and hands-on experiments.

AV² was built to bridge the gap between print and digital. We encourage you to tell us what you like and what you want to see in the future.

Sign up to be an AV² Ambassador at www.av2books.com/ambassador.